Feel Better, Little Buddy

Feel Better, Little Buddy

Animals with Casts

Julia Segal

CHRONICLE BOOKS

SAN FRANCISCO

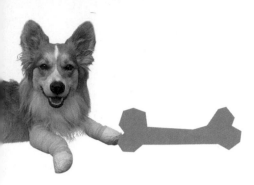

Library of Congress Cataloging-in-Publication Data;
Segal, Julia.
  Feel better, little buddy : animals with casts / Julia Segal.
    p. cm.
  ISBN 978-0-8118-7760-2 (pbk.)
 1. Pets—Wounds and injuries—Treatment. 2. Pets—Wounds and
injuries—Treatment—Pictorial works. 3. Surgical casts—Pictorial works.
4. Pets—Pictorial works. I. Title.
  SF981.S44 2011
  636.089'710222—dc22

Manufactured in China

Designed by Suzanne LaGasa
Design assistance by Cat Grishaver

10 9 8 7 6 5 4 3 2 1

Chronicle Books LLC
680 Second Street
San Francisco, California 94107
www.chroniclebooks.com

This book is dedicated to anyone who has ever helped an animal (with a cast or without) and to my family, who taught me to be one of those people.

Unless someone like you cares a whole awful lot, nothing is going to get better. It's not.

~Dr. Seuss

introduction

Animals with Casts

Most people see the words "animals with casts" and think "How cute" and "How awful" at the same time.

Don't worry; that's a natural reaction. Adorable sadness and helpless cuteness is a potent combination. Though the animals in this book are not at their peak of physical fitness, they are all on the road to recovery. My hope is that *Feel Better, Little Buddy* will appeal to people who think the little critters are just too darn cute, no matter what, as well as to kids and adults who might be dealing with an injury and all the frustrations that come with it.

Sometimes it's nice to see that even puppies and parakeets need to depend on the care and kindness of their loved ones to get them through a tough time. This may sound like your friend's hippie mom talking, but as anyone who has loved an animal—whether a dog, a rat, a cat, a horse, or a bunny rabbit—can tell you, animals have feelings and emotions, and witnessing them evokes a strong emotional connection that inspires and comforts us.

Some of my favorite stories are from doctors at children's hospitals. Pictures of animals in casts and recovering from injuries bring comfort to kids who are injured and scared to be in a cast. From a minor boo-boo to a broken leg, such accidents can seem much better when you see a picture of an adorable pug going through the same ordeal!

Many of the photos in this book are from animal rescue organizations, which submitted pictures of their injured animals, ranging from exotic animals (the three-toed sloth!) to the common household pet. Through these pictures, we hope to raise awareness of the organizations and rescuers who dedicate themselves to the selfless cause of helping wounded animals recover.

From the ridiculously adorable to the bizarrely cute and downright scruffy, all the animals with casts in the following photographs have a fighting, life-loving, and enduring spirit, which they share with the humans who love them.

NAME: Dusty

CAREGIVER: Frankie O'Connor

HOMETOWN: San Diego, California

This little fighter was three months old when he tussled with a fourteen-year-old cat, who was about five times his weight. The wrestling match ended with Dusty breaking a kneecap. Don't worry; he's fine. We even have an updated picture of him to prove it!

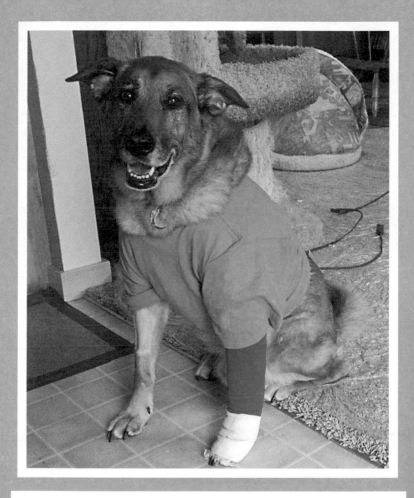

NAME: Bear
CAREGIVER: Melissa R. Weintraub
HOMETOWN: Corvallis, Oregon

Bear had a large tumor on his leg that had to be operated on. He recently had his year-and-a-half follow-up appointment, which went very well with no evidence of any return of the tumor. Bear just turned thirteen a couple of weeks ago and, from what we hear, remains an overgrown puppy!

NAME: Mariah and Zip
CAREGIVER: Sloth Sanctuary of Costa Rica
HOMETOWN: Limon, Costa Rica

This Bradypus (three-toed sloth) arrived at the Sloth Sanctuary of Costa Rica with a broken arm and a baby on board. Momma was able to return to the wild after four months of healing and rehabilitation, but Zip remains at the sanctuary as a permanent resident. He spent those four months in the clinic with his mom as she continued to nurse him, which meant during that time he was not out in the forest learning from his mother how to be a successful wild sloth. A baby sloth stays with its mother, hanging on to her chest and tummy as she forages about the jungle, for up to a year. Though Zip missed out on that opportunity, he has a pretty sweet life at the sanctuary. Next time you're in Costa Rica, stop by for a visit!

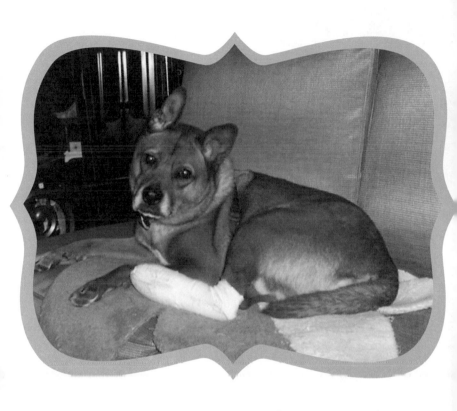

NAME: Logan
CAREGIVER: Kay Fredrick
HOMETOWN: Indianapolis, Indiana

NAME: Juno
CAREGIVER: Heidi Smith
HOMETOWN: Alfred, Maine

Juno is a Lab/weimaraner mix. She is seen here wearing casts and what her owner calls the "cone of shame."

NAME: Cricket
CAREGIVER: Marty Ambos
HOMETOWN: Chicago, Illinois

She was probably a bit annoyed with her name when she broke her elbow and couldn't even joke about hopping around for a few weeks.

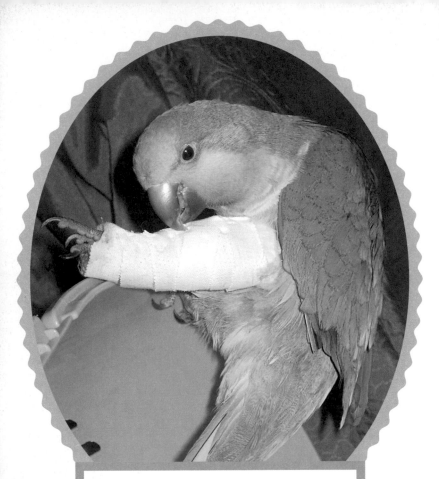

NAME: Adrian

CAREGIVER: Yasi Dinatale

HOMETOWN: Portland, Oregon

He may look like a sad birdie here, but Adrian, a Quaker parrot, happily found out that his broken leg was misdiagnosed, and the cast came off a few days later.

NAME: Abbey

CAREGIVER: Michael Beck

HOMETOWN: Highland, Michigan

NAME: Dan

CAREGIVER: Rich Bailey

HOMETOWN: Seattle, Washington

Dan did NOT like the bandage in this picture, so that lasted only for a little bit.

NAME: Milo

CAREGIVER: Jeff Harris

HOMETOWN: New York City, New York

Mr. Grumpypants wasn't having the greatest day when this picture was taken, but he is back to being a happy dog.

NAME: Hans

CAREGIVER: Suzann Janvrin

HOMETOWN: Tampa, Florida

Hans is a Flemish Giant rabbit. His owners got him when he was four months old. Soon after, he broke his arm. Despite the cast, he enjoyed being held like the big baby he is.

NAME: Rory

CAREGIVER: Andrew Gartrell

HOMETOWN: San Francisco, California

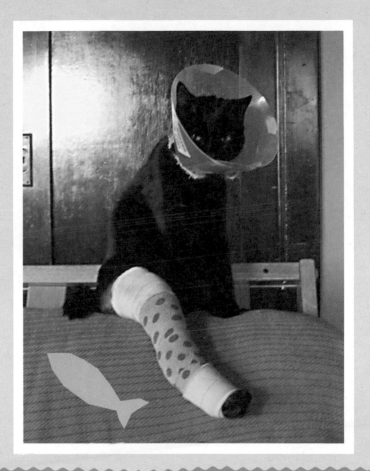

NAME: Blackie

CAREGIVER: Natalie Lawler

HOMETOWN: Los Angeles, California

This tough girl got herself into a series of neighborhood rumbles and ended up with several casts at different times over the course of three months. This is one of her mellow moments while on her fifth cast, which is pretty much as street legit as a cat can get.

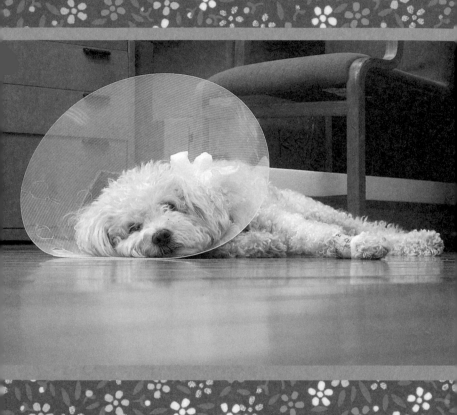

NAME: Zoe

CAREGIVER: Jillian Salik

HOMETOWN: New York City, New York

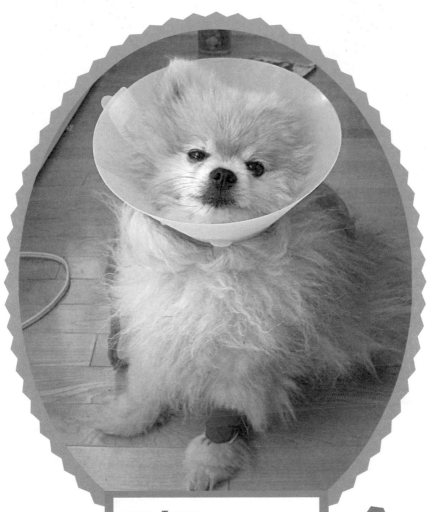

NAME: Tommy
CAREGIVER: Mackenzie Kosut
HOMETOWN: Brooklyn, New York

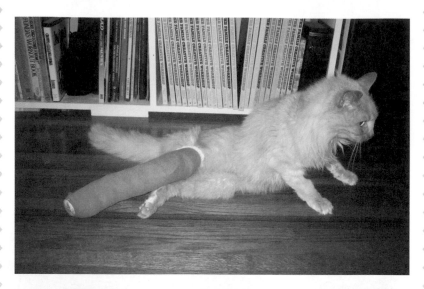

NAME: Joaquin

CAREGIVER: Elizabeth Herndon

HOMETOWN: Los Angeles, California

Joaquin broke his leg a few years ago, and his owner couldn't stop taking photos of him in his various colored casts. Too cute!

NAME: Mike

CAREGIVER: Kris Kiedis

HOMETOWN: Orlando, Florida

NAME: Biscuit

CAREGIVER: Anne Sullivan and Nemo Hoffman

HOMETOWN: Brooklyn, New York

Biscuit jumped over a fence and cut his toe open on the way. No more dog-gang initiations for him.

NAME: Thistle

CAREGIVER: Nicole Hamilton

HOMETOWN: Victoria, British Columbia, Canada

Thistle, a little hedgehog from Victoria, Canada, has a bad foot infection. But he makes even a foot infection seem adorable.

NAME: Albie

CAREGIVER: Maryam Shariat

HOMETOWN: Oakland, California

Albie had surgery on his paw and wore a cast for a week. Some animals seem to get embarrassed by their casts, so Albie's owners tried to make his cast look like a sneaker so he wouldn't be so self-conscious.

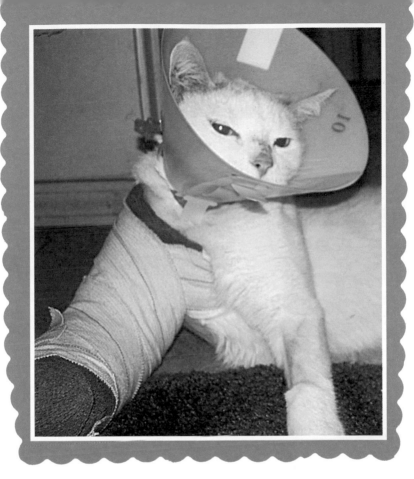

NAME: Steven Patrick

CAREGIVER: Liz Ortega

HOMETOWN: La Mirada, California

Steven Patrick after falling off the roof . . .
that's the last time he puts up the Christmas
lights by himself!

NAME: Lula-Belle

CAREGIVER: Mike Goodwin

HOMETOWN: Dallas, Texas

Lula-Belle in her cast. We hear she made a complete recovery and is back terrorizing all the neighborhood squirrels. Good girl!

NAME: Baylor

CAREGIVER: Allison Cate

HOMETOWN: Nashville, Tennessee

This little prankster fell down the stairs
just in time for Halloween.

NAME: Chester

CAREGIVER: Debbie Meadows

HOMETOWN: Virginia Beach, Virginia

NAME: Chloe

CAREGIVER: Karen Sweet

HOMETOWN: Northern Alabama

Chloe knows she can't do keyboard cat reenactments at parties for a while.

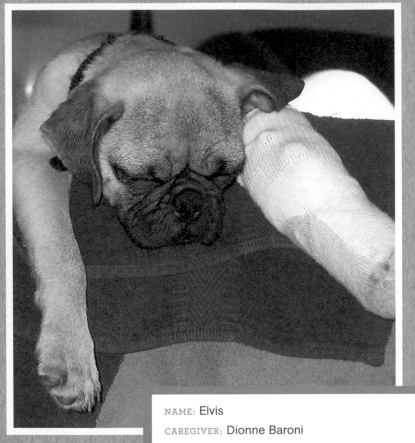

NAME: Elvis

CAREGIVER: Dionne Baroni

HOMETOWN: Escondido, California

According to his owner, Elvis is a really chilled-out, laid-back dog. Even in this huge cast, Elvis was a trouper.

NAME: Harry Truman

CAREGIVER: Jason Coleman

HOMETOWN: Richmond, Virginia

Maggie, the owner's newest dog, doesn't seem to realize that she's about 2½ times the size of Harry. Harry decided not to press doggie charges.

NAME: **Waffle**

CAREGIVER: **Megan Hughes**

HOMETOWN: **Simi Valley, California**

This baby bunny named Waffle broke her
leg and got a bright pink cast. She also got
a cute award from us.

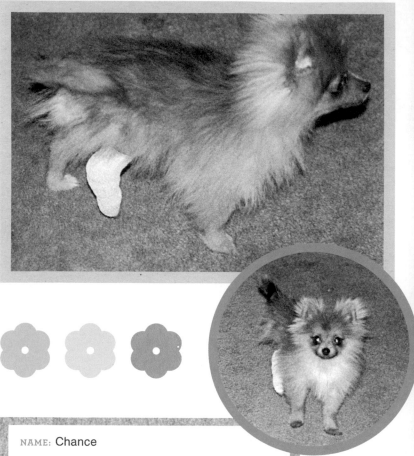

NAME: Chance

CAREGIVER: Katherine Cooper and Caleb Lee

HOMETOWN: Evans, Georgia

This is Chance when he was six months old.
His big sister accidentally broke his leg! He
had to have a wire and pins placed to fix it. . . .
He likes to think he is now Robo-dog.

NAME: Lulu

CAREGIVER: Candee F. Scott

HOMETOWN: Oklahoma City, Oklahoma

NAME: Tosca

CAREGIVER: Cecile Bazant

HOMETOWN: Cologne, Germany

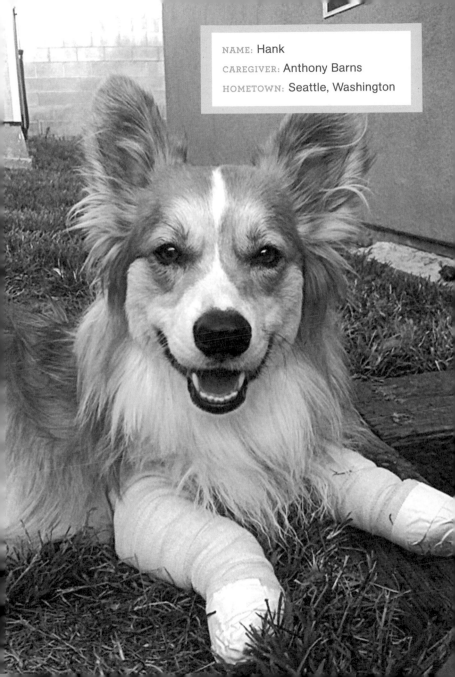

NAME: Hank
CAREGIVER: Anthony Barns
HOMETOWN: Seattle, Washington

NAME: Zoie

CAREGIVER: Sherry Wieland

HOMETOWN: Gilbert, Arizona

NAME: Chucky

CAREGIVER: Roxy Duarte

HOMETOWN: Austin, Texas

The Chuckster has had so many surgeries
that his owners call him the million-dollar kitty!
Doesn't he look . . . mad? (But also really cute?)

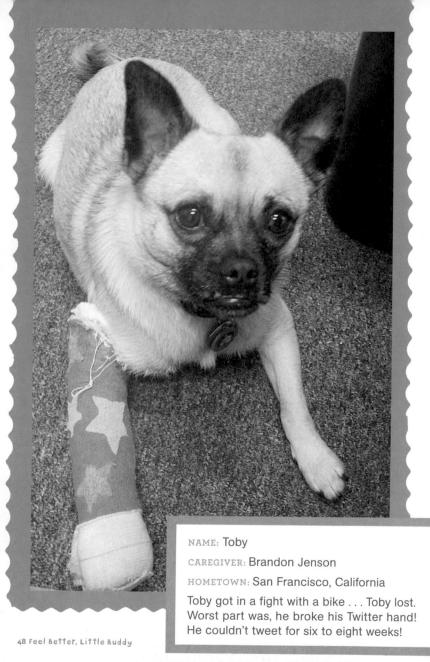

NAME: Toby

CAREGIVER: Brandon Jenson

HOMETOWN: San Francisco, California

Toby got in a fight with a bike . . . Toby lost. Worst part was, he broke his Twitter hand! He couldn't tweet for six to eight weeks!

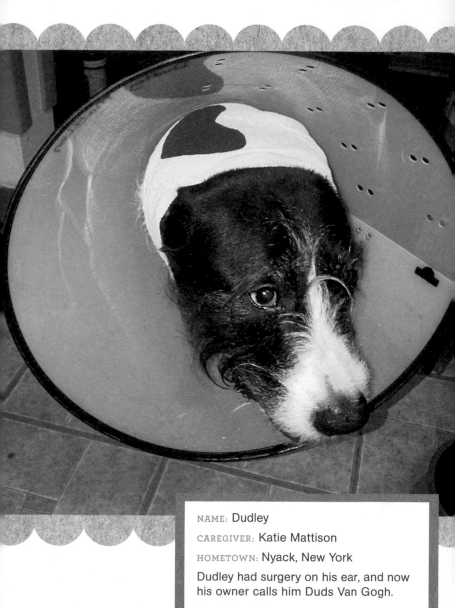

NAME: Dudley

CAREGIVER: Katie Mattison

HOMETOWN: Nyack, New York

Dudley had surgery on his ear, and now his owner calls him Duds Van Gogh.

NAME: Lars

CAREGIVER: Kathleen Bennett

HOMETOWN: Seattle, Washington

Lars has two favorite hobbies: kicking ass and chewing gum . . . and it looks as if he is all out of gum.

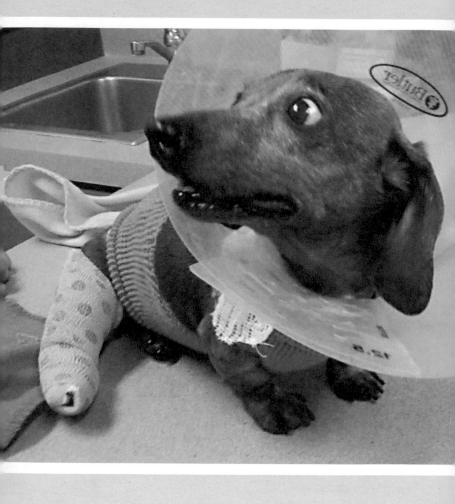

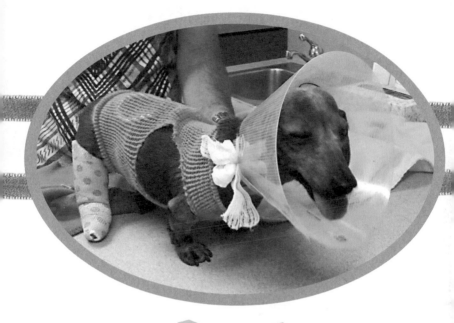

NAME: Heidi Lane

CAREGIVER: Lauren Archer

HOMETOWN: Burbank, California

NAME: George

CAREGIVER: Rachel Chamberlin

HOMETOWN: New York City, New York

George was six weeks old and his owner had had him for less than twenty-four hours when a pile of boxes collapsed from the top shelf of a roommate's closet onto the two-pound kitten! Luckily, after surgery and a month in a cast, he was all better!

NAME: Peanut

CAREGIVER: Missy Lutz

HOMETOWN: Newberry, South Carolina

NAME: Popple

CAREGIVER: Rachel Forbes

HOMETOWN: Los Gatos, California

This Chinese crested puppy was about nine months old when she jumped out of her owner's arms onto the floor, breaking both of her tiny forearms. Her bones were too small for reconstructive surgery to be an option (she weighs only five pounds fully grown), so her owners had to put her two front legs in casts and hope they healed well. She was in the casts for more than three months, during which time she learned to walk around and jump up and down steps without using her front legs at all!

NAME: Grisette

CAREGIVER: Eric Delcroix

HOMETOWN: Lille, France

NAME: Pupp

CAREGIVER: Casey Kennan

HOMETOWN: Venice, Italy

NAME: Cookie

CAREGIVER: Brian King

HOMETOWN: De Pere, Wisconsin

NAME: Panuk

CAREGIVER: Silke and Hasenbande

HOMETOWN: Bochum, Germany

Panuk lost the wrestling match . . .
but he won the staring contest.

NAME: Max

CAREGIVER: Tracy Cook

HOMETOWN: Plymouth, Devon, United Kingdom

NAME: Lola

CAREGIVER: Meghan Mowery

HOMETOWN: Tustin, California

NAME: Lilly

CAREGIVER: Christi Finley

HOMETOWN: Seattle, Washington

Little Lilly has broken her leg twice and had two surgeries between the breaks. She is a cast regular! But a very cute one!

NAME: Pixel
CAREGIVER: Lisa Wong Jackson
HOMETOWN: Berkeley, California

NAME: Talullah

CAREGIVER: Samuel Chiszar and Ariel Braverman

HOMETOWN: New York City, New York

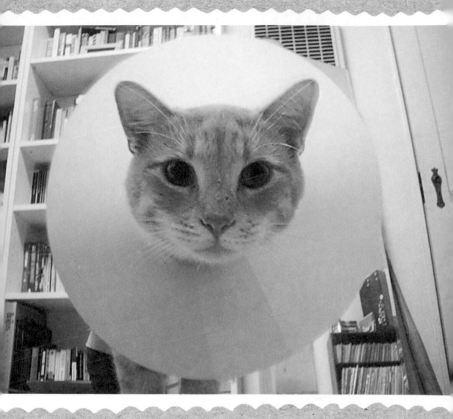

NAME: Oscar

CAREGIVER: Alice Handley

HOMETOWN: Oakland, California

It wasn't his brightest moment when Oscar tried to see if he could fly out of a third-floor window. He couldn't. He is better now and hopefully has learned that he is not a kitty superhero, especially without his cape on.

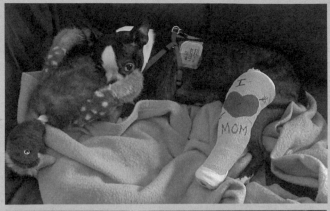

NAME: Costanza

CAREGIVER: Manuela Esposito

HOMETOWN: Stratford, Connecticut

This little Boston terrier was just six months old when he broke his leg tumbling down a flight of stairs chasing his big brother. He is fine now.

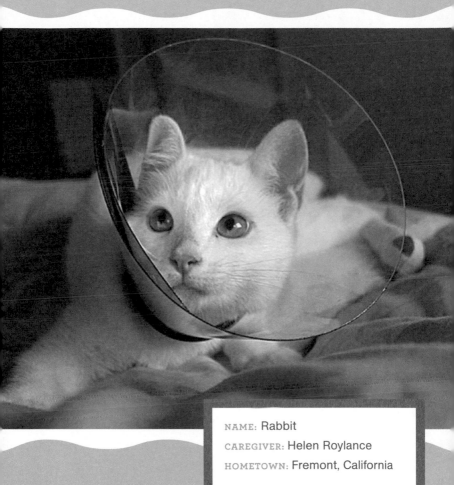

NAME: Rabbit

CAREGIVER: Helen Roylance

HOMETOWN: Fremont, California

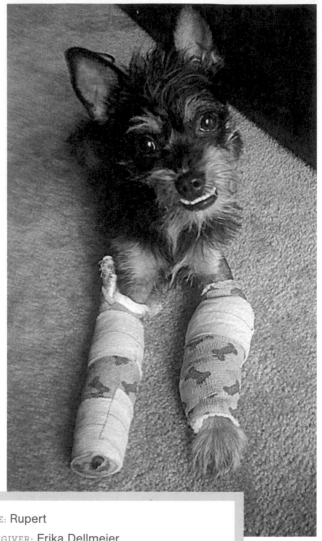

NAME: Rupert

CAREGIVER: Erika Dellmeier

HOMETOWN: Nashville, Tennessee

Rupert may have broken her front legs while filming the new *Mission: Impossible* dog movie . . . or she might be making that up.

NAME: Kitty

CAREGIVER: Jon Cardona

HOMETOWN: Oklahoma City, Oklahoma

NAME: Lucy Freetly
CAREGIVER: Adam Freetly
HOMETOWN: Austin, Texas

NAME: Stella

CAREGIVER: Vicki Arnold

HOMETOWN: Eldridge, Iowa

NAME: Sinbad

CAREGIVER: Allison Stedry

HOMETOWN: Boulder, Colorado.

Sinbad had an abscess on his paw, and, on top of that, the doctors had to put drops in his eyes to dilate them, making him that much more lovable.

NAME: Cooper and Sledge

CAREGIVER: Karri Dahl

HOMETOWN: Seattle, Washington

The cat had nothing to do with poor Cooper's injuries—she swears.

NAME: Pancake Sue (and Cassie)

CAREGIVER: Rachael Hetzel

HOMETOWN: Rochester, New York

Pancake Sue broke her toe, so, for a while, her name became Peg Leg Sue. The other dog in the picture is Cassie, and she is the one who broke Sue's toe. These two have hopefully gone through the emotional healing process of forgiveness and have become friends again. I wonder if that Thursday night doggie couple's therapy group is working . . .

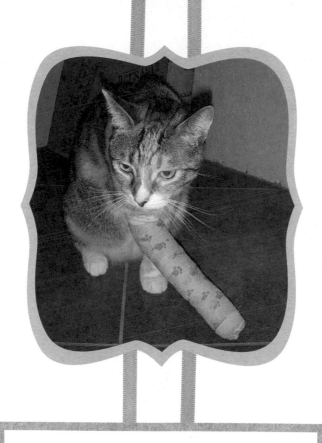

NAME: Penny

CAREGIVER: Megan Watson

HOMETOWN: Victoria, British Columbia, Canada

Penny the kitty broke one of her legs. She's all better now, and, yes, she cost her owner a few . . . pennies.

NAME: Phoenix

CAREGIVER: Jen Chamberlain

HOMETOWN: New York City, New York

Phoenix will never wear Christian Louboutin six-inch heels in the rain ever again!

NAME: Roxie

CAREGIVER: Julia Weiskopf

HOMETOWN: New York City, New York

Roxie fractured her leg and had to have metal plates put in. Her owner says she is a bionic puppy.

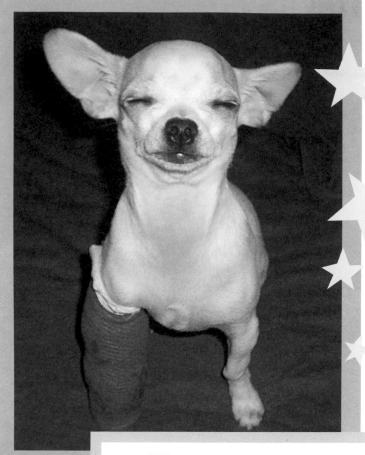

NAME: Eddy

CAREGIVER: Jennifer Cordova

HOMETOWN: Canton, Oklahoma

"I caan haz Vvicoden!?" Yeah, this little guy is thoroughly enjoying his painkiller medication. This photo was taken after he was treated for a fracture in his tiny paw.

NAME: Point

CAREGIVER: Zhelez Atanasov and Stanimira Boeva

HOMETOWN: Varna, Bulgaria

NAME: Scraggles

CAREGIVER: Emily Nathon

HOMETOWN: Los Angeles, California

NAME: Puck

CAREGIVER: Amanda Heuermann

HOMETOWN: Chicago, Illinois

This rabbit sprained his ankle and was in a cast for several weeks. He's fine now and hops without a limp. Still has a badass attitude, though. Some things never change.

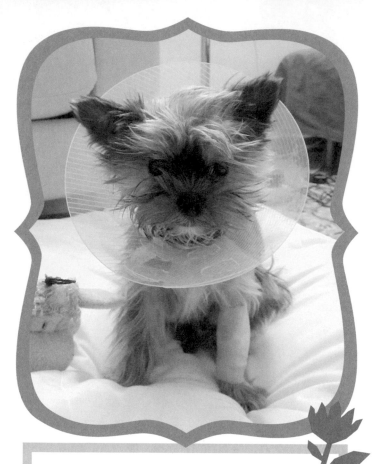

NAME: Tito

CAREGIVER: Matt Klein

HOMETOWN: Prague, Czech Republic

The cute patrol is about to pull this doggy over for excessive cuteness. As if Tito wasn't sweet enough, he's from Prague in the Czech Republic! Dogs with exotic accents are a whole new level of lovable.

NAME: Sammy

CAREGIVER: Cathy O'Brien

HOMETOWN: Cincinnati, Ohio

This little guy isn't exactly loving his pink cast.
But if looks could kill. . . . Don't worry, Sammy,
pink is the new black.

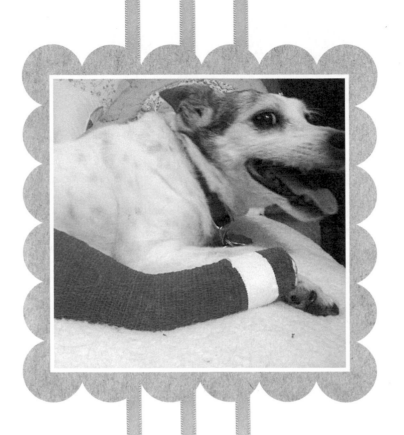

NAME: Squirt

CAREGIVER: Heather Scott

HOMETOWN: Austin, Texas

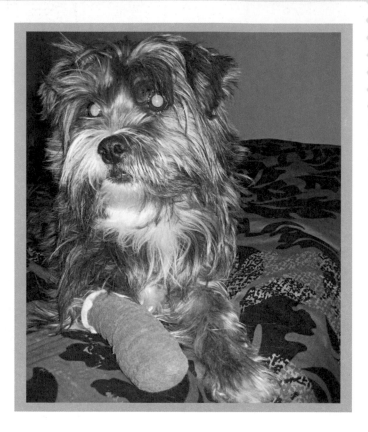

NAME: Teddy

CAREGIVER: Eric Grannan

HOMETOWN: Riverside, California

This little guy is all better, but now he sometimes shows babes this picture to show them how tough he is!

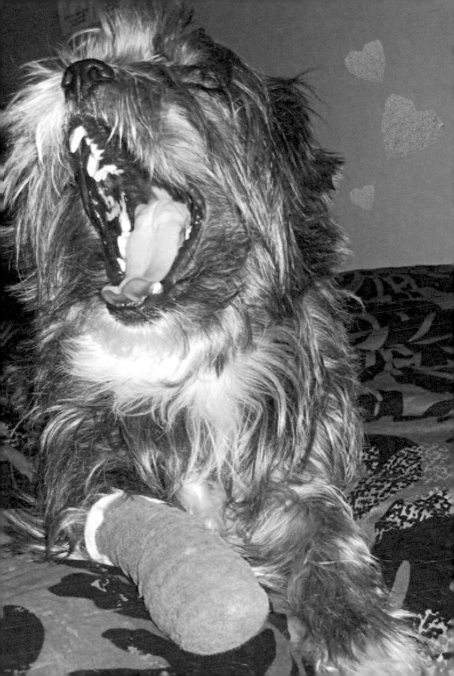

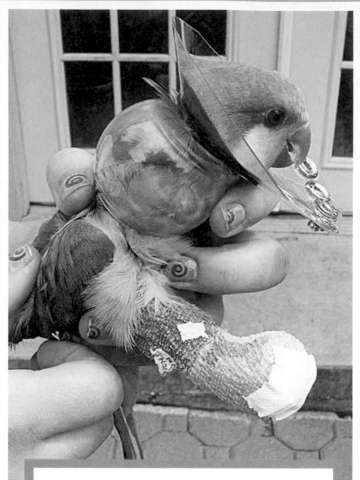

NAME: Rufio

CAREGIVER: Jessica Gilzow

HOMETOWN: Austin, Texas

Rufio here needed a cast—he also wanted to look like a bird astronaut. He has gray on his feathers because he is getting older . . . doesn't that sound familiar?

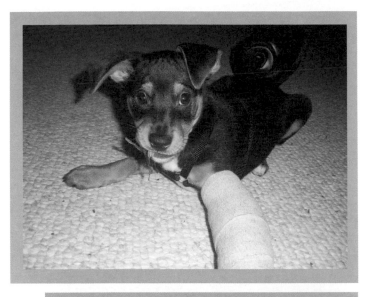

NAME: Ziggy

CAREGIVER: Chelsea Lane

HOMETOWN: Chicago, Illinois

NAME: Roo

CAREGIVER: Kristine Tofte

HOMETOWN: Austin, Texas

This sugar glider had to have the tips of two of her back left toes amputated. She is doing better now—look at her adorable face!

NAME: Penny

CAREGIVER: Evan Solocek

HOMETOWN: Milwaukee, Wisconsin

NAME: Rugby

CAREGIVER: Christine A. Miller

HOMETOWN: Dallastown, Pennsylvania

This American bulldog initially had a green cast after he broke his leg. In the end, it took a pin, steel rigging, and two years to straighten the bone, but Rugby's all better now.

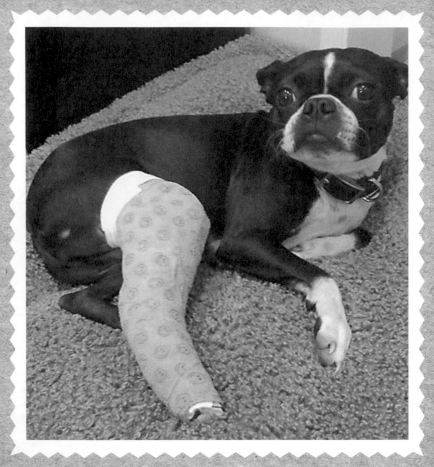

NAME: Obi

CAREGIVER: Justin Giritlian

HOMETOWN: Los Angeles, California

Last year, Obi broke his tibia. After having a metal plate installed, he is back to chasing squirrels and climbing trees, but this is what he looked while he was getting better.

NAME: Doc

CAREGIVER: Rebecca Sundermeier

HOMETOWN: Manhattan, Kansas

Poor little Doc. He got stitches, he had to be in a cone, and he had to hear all those bad "your name's Doc, but you needed one" jokes.

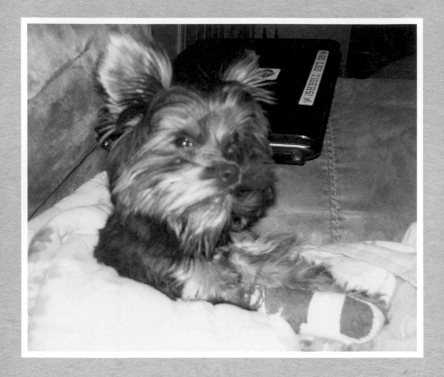

NAME: Monster

CAREGIVER: Ruby Dorroh

HOMETOWN: Denham Springs, Louisiana

Monster may look small, but she is all about attitude. BIG attitude.

NAME: Rex
CAREGIVER: Kate Trainor
HOMETOWN: New Mexico

NAME: Fergie

CAREGIVER: Sonja Gentry

HOMETOWN: Phoenix, Arizona

This Pembroke Welsh Corgi is named Fergie.
She injured her foot on a fence but is now
completely healed and doing fabulously.

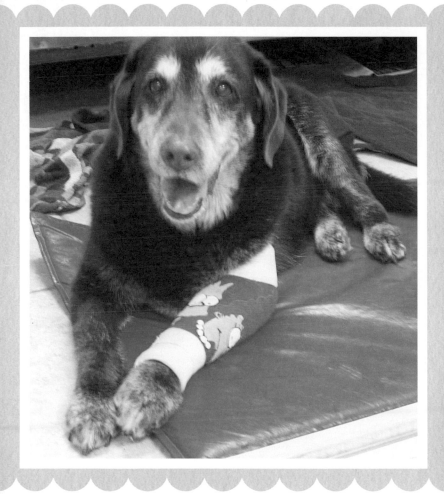

NAME: Molly Miller

CAREGIVER: Andrea Komkov, DVM

HOMETOWN: Dallas, Texas

NAME: Bodie

CAREGIVER: Gabriela Mor

HOMETOWN: Davie, Florida

This chihuahua looks about as happy as that time somebody said, "¡Yo quiero Taco Bell!" to him.

NAME: Kiwi

CAREGIVER: Cassandra Delvey

HOMETOWN: Mission Viejo, California

Kiwi is coming back after an overnight stay at the vet for pancreatitis. He came back with these smiley-face bandages and a smile on his face! He looks happy to be home!

NAME: Dio

CAREGIVER: M. Chavez

HOMETOWN: Upland, California

NAME: Molly

CAREGIVER: Dena Davis

HOMETOWN: Barrington, Rhode Island

NAME: Lucy

CAREGIVER: Chris Lourenco

HOMETOWN: Boston, Massachusetts

Even with a cast, Lucy poses like a supermodel.

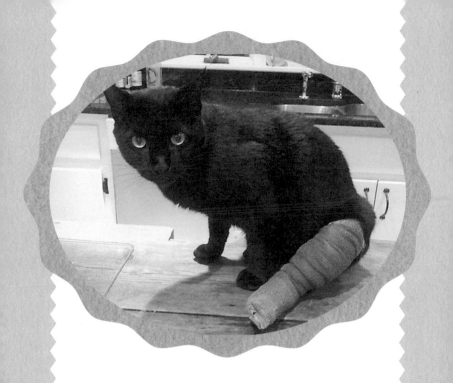

NAME: Murphy

CAREGIVER: Quinn Rose Levine

HOMETOWN: New York City, New York

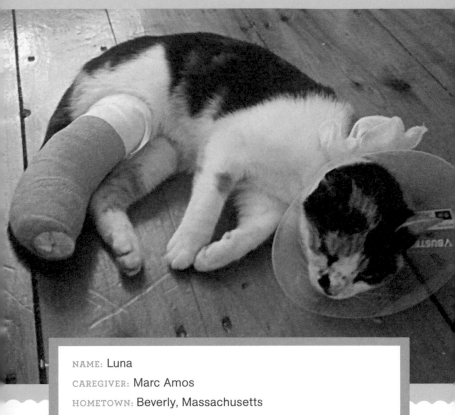

NAME: Luna

CAREGIVER: Marc Amos

HOMETOWN: Beverly, Massachusetts

Luna hurt herself outdoors. Nobody knows how she did it specifically, but the vet says that she'll be fine and that she now has the most expensive leg in the neighborhood.

NAME: Gracie

CAREGIVER: Peggy Shanks

HOMETOWN: Kingston, Ontario, Canada

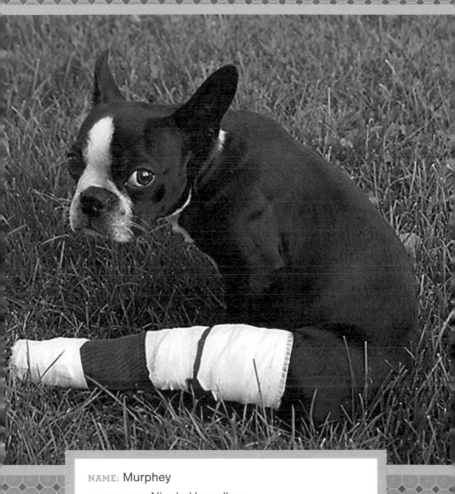

NAME: Murphey

CAREGIVER: Nicole Vangellow

HOMETOWN: Potsdam, New York

After getting beaten up by a cat, little Murph here learned a good lesson: Watch out for those claws.

NAME: Lulubelle

CAREGIVER: Jennifer Coyle

HOMETOWN: Los Angeles, California

NAME: Carrot
CAREGIVER: Brice Lovell
HOMETOWN: Washington DC

NAME: Diego

CAREGIVER: Emily Spurlock

HOMETOWN: Sterling Heights, Michigan

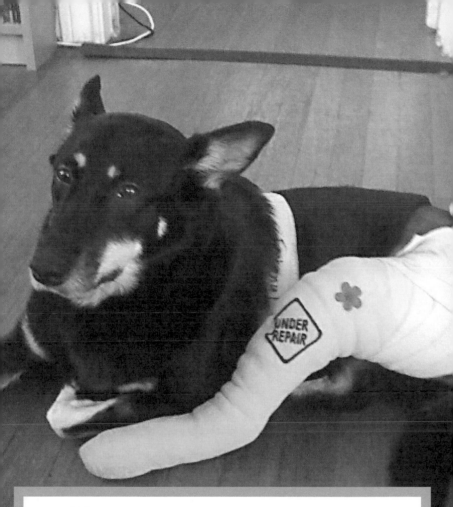

NAME: Nola

CAREGIVER: David Jack Browning

HOMETOWN: Houston, Texas

This little cutie lives in Houston, but is named after her owner's last place of residence. Nola got this cast due to an anterior cruciate rupture (a knee injury). It may have put a damper on her NFL Super Bowl rushing title—but it won't stop her for long.

NAME: Madison

CAREGIVER: Erin Leigh

HOMETOWN: Seattle, Washington

Madison was hit by a car and broke both front legs.
But thanks to his vet, he doesn't even have a limp.
The skull-and-crossbones cast looked cool, and now
Madison is back to running around, tough as ever.

NAME: Winston

CAREGIVER: The Griffith Family

HOMETOWN: Virginia Beach, Virginia

NAME: David

CAREGIVER: Audrey Fisher at the
Bideawee Adoption Center

HOMETOWN: New York City, New York

NAME: Rocky

CAREGIVER: Gary Friend

HOMETOWN: Chevy Chase, Maryland

NAME: Earnest Mittens
CAREGIVER: Elisabeth Tysse and Shanty Dwellers
HOMETOWN: Arlington, Virginia

NAME: Megan Marie

CAREGIVER: Catherine Bruhn

HOMETOWN: Spring Branch, Texas

NAME: Jellybean

CAREGIVER: Laura Joan Brickley

HOMETOWN: Louisville, Kentucky

The only way Jellybean could look any cuter is if she were riding a unicorn with a cast.

NAME: Libby

CAREGIVER: Melissa Sullivan and the Sullivan Family

HOMETOWN: Brockton, Massachusetts

This sweet girl cut two tendons, so her vet decided to add a message to her cast. Her owners think she's starting to like it since she gets all of the attention she wants!

NAME: Grey

CAREGIVER: Maria Rapier

HOMETOWN: Brooklyn, New York

Grey got his cast because he was injured while beating up a shark . . . well, that's what he tells the ladies.

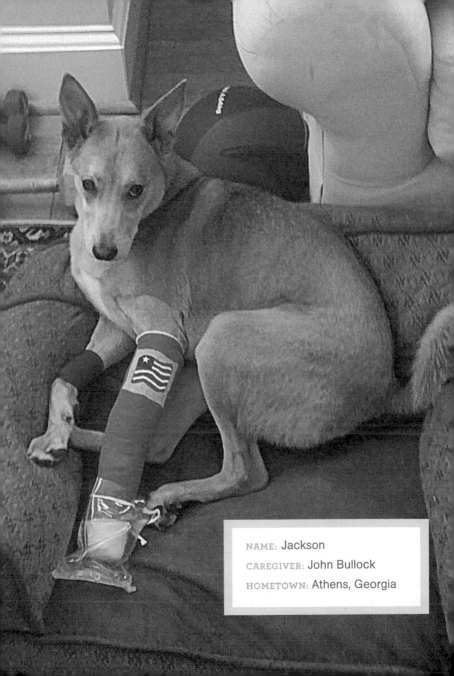

NAME: Jackson

CAREGIVER: John Bullock

HOMETOWN: Athens, Georgia

NAME: Hopper

CAREGIVER: Craig Kasprzak

HOMETOWN: Miami, Florida

NAME: Chloe

CAREGIVER: Christina Bohn

HOMETOWN: Port Jefferson, New York

This is Chloe. She tore her Achilles tendon and was cast-bound for six weeks. It hasn't stopped her from giving kisses though!

NAME: Chibo

CAREGIVER: Ankesh Kadakia

HOMETOWN: Portland, Oregon

NAME: Jake

CAREGIVER: Elaina

HOMETOWN: Charlotte, North Carolina

. . . and you thought Garfield had an attitude.

NAME: Jasper

CAREGIVER: Natile Quebodeaux

HOMETOWN: Lafayette, Louisiana

This is Jasper and his pig, Volterra. This picture was taken right after he got out of the puppy ER.

NAME: Bradley

CAREGIVER: Caitlin McMahon

HOMETOWN: Sudbury, Massachusetts

Bradley had a run-in with a car, but it looks like he's back on the road to recovery. Bradley thought that was a bad joke, too.

NAME: Jewel

CAREGIVER: Judy Avey-Arroyo

HOMETOWN: Limon, Costa Rica

Jewel is a Bradypus—a.k.a. a sloth. She was just a baby when she arrived at the Sloth Sanctuary of Costa Rica with a broken arm. After sanctuary caretakers put the cast on, Judie, the sanctuary owner's nine-year-old granddaughter, said, "Oh, Nana, she looks like a jewel!" The name suits Jewel very well.

NAME: Dolly

CAREGIVER: Susan Mouras

HOMETOWN: Boston, Massachusetts

Dolly fell through a lounge chair, which is the opposite of relaxing.

NAME: Cia

CAREGIVER: Daniel Hofstadter

HOMETOWN: San Francisco, California

This little lady had surgery on both legs last year. She's doing fine now, her owner says. It looks as if it was tough for her to get around and yet easy for her to be adorable.

NAME: Georgie

CAREGIVER: Jason Allgood

HOMETOWN: Chicago, Illinois

Poor Georgie. He was in a cast for about twelve weeks and was about to get out when this picture was taken. He looks so happy!

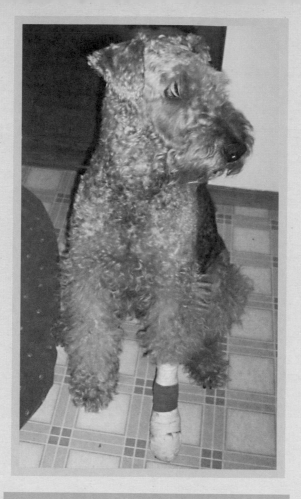

NAME: Easton

CAREGIVER: Cassy Daigneau

HOMETOWN: Tilbury, Ontario, Canada

Easton is an Airedale terrier, who broke his toe while chasing a squirrel. Looking at his face, he might be deciding if it was worth it.

NAME: Jim

CAREGIVER: Marianne Prince

HOMETOWN: Carrboro, North Carolina

Meet Jim (who is actually a hen). She survived a dog attack, which is a pretty tough thing to do, so don't call her chicken.

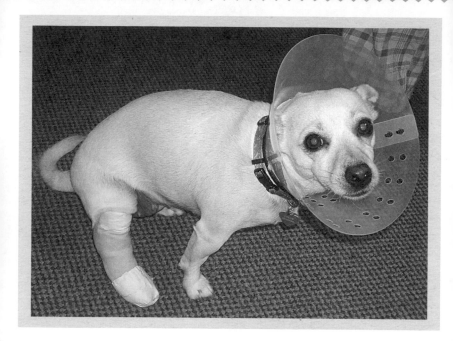

NAME: Chloe Sue

CAREGIVER: Isabel Ogden

HOMETOWN: San Diego, California

Who likes being in a cast? Nobody. But even animals have to deal with it, and they sometimes wear these collars so they don't try to gnaw off their casts! Who can blame them?

NAME: Biff

CAREGIVER: Heidi Smith

HOMETOWN: Jamaica Plain, Massachusetts

Biff broke his kitty paw going through a doggie door on a dare from the family hamster. It's a long story, and to tell the truth Biff would rather we all forget about the whole thing.

NAME: Cocoa Bean

CAREGIVER: Katie Beckman

HOMETOWN: Falls Church, Virginia

This super-shaggy mini poodle had just been adopted when she had an accident. It gave her and her owner some quality time to get to know each other.

NAME: Cindy

CAREGIVER: Jorge Mexicano

HOMETOWN: Mexico City, Mexico

If this little thing were any sweeter, she would give you cavities.

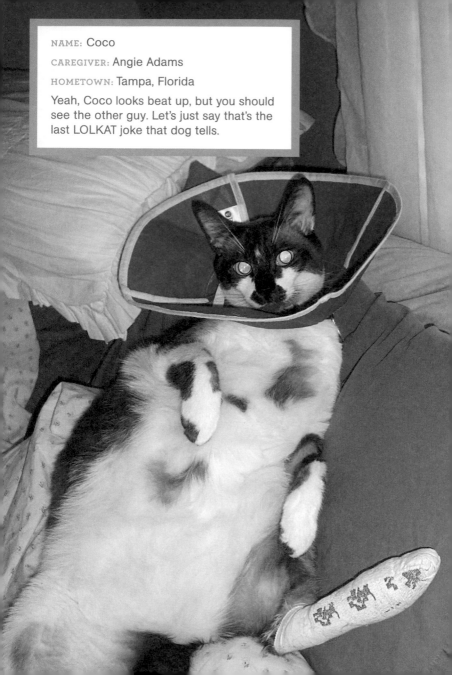

NAME: Coco

CAREGIVER: Angie Adams

HOMETOWN: Tampa, Florida

Yeah, Coco looks beat up, but you should see the other guy. Let's just say that's the last LOLKAT joke that dog tells.

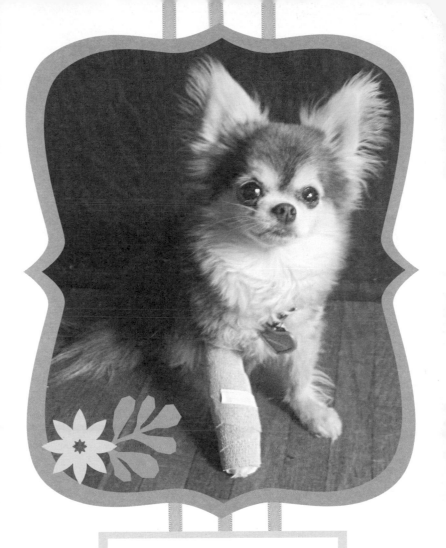

NAME: Bluey
CAREGIVER: Adria Richards
HOMETOWN: Minneapolis, Minnesota

NAME: Shelley

CAREGIVER: Lauran Vohmann

HOMETOWN: Guernsey, United Kingdom

It's sad that you can't hug a tortoise the way you can a puppy. Shelly is so cute you might just try, though! If she hides, try kissing her shell.

NAME: Snow
CAREGIVER: Laura Guerette
HOMETOWN: Quebec, Canada

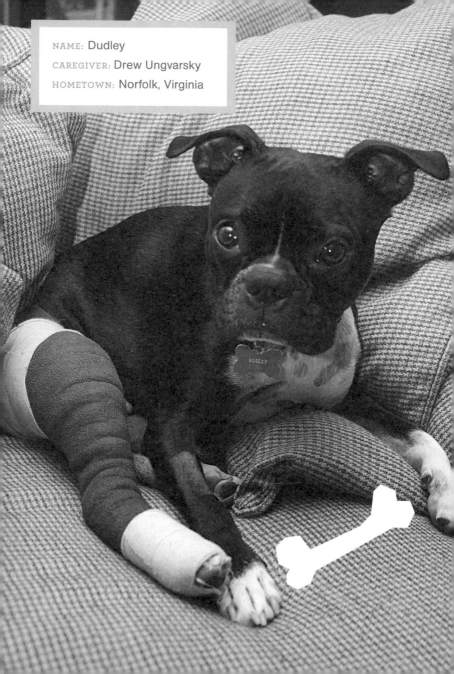

NAME: Cooper

CAREGIVER: Stacey D. Joslin

HOMETOWN: New York City, New York

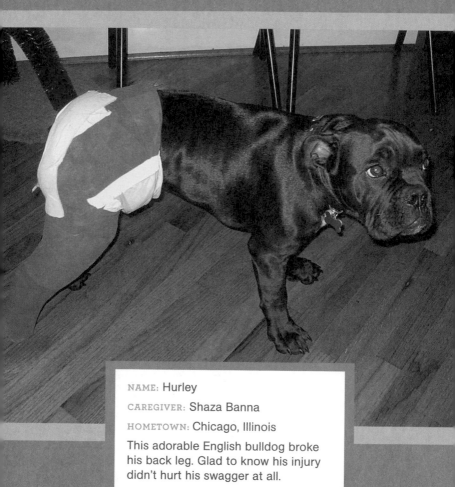

NAME: Hurley

CAREGIVER: Shaza Banna

HOMETOWN: Chicago, Illinois

This adorable English bulldog broke his back leg. Glad to know his injury didn't hurt his swagger at all.

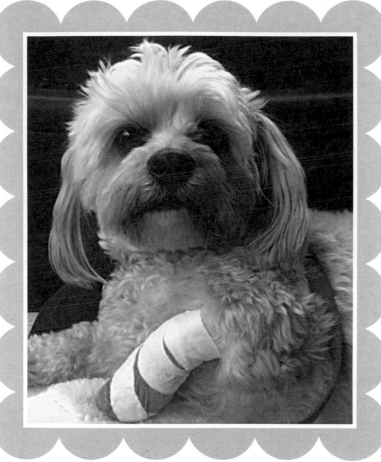

NAME: Lucky

CAREGIVER: Matthew Dennis

HOMETOWN: Los Angeles, California

NAME: Roxy

CAREGIVER: Nicole Sundquist

HOMETOWN: Moscow, Idaho

NAME: Zena

CAREGIVER: The Donkey Sanctuary

HOMETOWN: Devon, England

This foal's name is Zena, and she lives at the Donkey Sanctuary, which is based in England and helps donkeys all over the world. Zena's legs were cast in an attempt to give her added strength in standing to reach her mother's milk. As you can see, she is doing better every day thanks to the staff's great care. Come visit her and say "Hi!"

NAME: Barkley

CAREGIVER: Molly Thibault

HOMETOWN: Santa Barbara, California

Acknowledgments

I have to start by sincerely thanking every person who took the time to send me their animal pictures and stories. A big thanks to all of those people who take time to volunteer, donate to animal causes, and generally care for and help animals. I owe much gratitude to animal shelters and rescue and rehabilitation programs for taking the time to send in their pictures and share their stories with me. In particular, I would like to thank a few organizations and people that help animals every day—Audrey Fisher at the Bideawee Adoption Center (Bideawee. org); Judy Avey-Arroyo at the Sloth Sanctuary of Costa Rica (Slothrescue.org); Everyone at Safe Haven Rabbit Rescue (Savehavenrr.org); Cathy O'Brien at the STAF No-Kill Shelter (Staf.org); Andrea Komkov, DVM, and Karen Vanderloo, DVM. I'd also like to thank Dr. Anna Manolopoulos in Melbourne, who helps run a pediatric fracture clinic. She contacted me to share stories of how these cute pictures help children to be more at ease when having casts removed.

Many thanks also to the following folks, who gave me invaluable advice and encouragement: Brian Steinberg at Principato Young Entertainment; Rebecca Olivier at William Morris Endeavor Entertainment; and Joseph Veltre at the Veltre Company. Thanks to everyone at Chronicle: Christina Amini, who was the first person to start me going on this book; Emily Haynes; Emilie Sandoz; and everyone else I never got a chance to talk with directly, but who put in so much work and effort—I appreciate everything you have done for this book. I want to thank my parents, Nathan and Debbie, and everyone in the Segal and Humenik families for their support through the years, especially my brother David— thank you for being such an encouraging, caring brother. Your comedy and writing inspire me constantly. Finally, to all my friends in NYC and all over the world, thank you for all your help, for getting my sense of humor, and for making me feel endlessly loved and supported.